Managing Your Amazon Cloud Drive

All You Need to Know About Easy Cloud Storage

Disclaimer

No part of this eBook can be transmitted or reproduced in any form including print, electronic, photocopying, scanning, mechanical or recording without prior written permission from the author.

All information, ideas and guidelines presented here are for educational purposes only.

While the author has taken utmost efforts to ensure the accuracy of the written content, all readers are advised to follow information mentioned herein at their own risk. The author cannot be held responsible for any personal or commercial damage caused by misinterpretation of information. All readers are encouraged to seek professional advice when needed.

Contents

Summary

Whether they are your precious photos or files you cannot afford to lose, with Amazon Cloud Drive, they can be securely stored and always be at hand.

Access your important files or precious memories on the go when all your data is securely stored on cloud at Amazon Cloud Drive. This book covers all important aspects of managing your Amazon Cloud Drive and how this platform can be used effectively.

Amazon Cloud Drive makes storing your documents, videos, photos and other digital files in the Cloud easy and quick. Download today and get started with free storage that is available up to 5 G – the perfect place to store up to more than 2000 pictures at a time.

Read till the end and experience your Amazon Cloud Drive like never before.

Introduction – What is Cloud Drive?

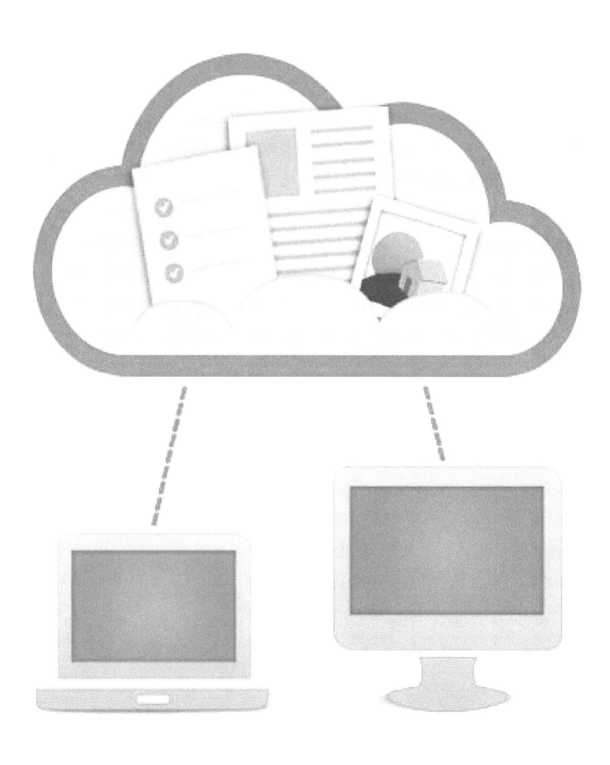

If you wish to enjoy your own personal storage space in the cloud, there is no other better option than Amazon Cloud Drive. This is an online hard drive where you can store your documents, videos, photos and more on the secure server of Amazon.

The browsers that support Amazon Cloud Drives include Internet Explorer (version 8 or above), Safari, Chrome, and Firefox (latest versions).

To enjoy the complete features of this amazing Cloud Drive, upgrade your browser to the latest version and make the most out of this opportunity.

Moreover, in order to run Cloud Drive effectively, you must also have JavaScript and Adobe Flash Player installed in your computer.

Music can also be stored in your Cloud Drive in the specified Music folder. However, with the introduction of Cloud Player Premium, you music is automatically moved to Archived Music folder.

Music that was stored in the Cloud Drive before the introduction of Cloud Player Premium, does not count against the storage quota of your Cloud Drive.

Enjoy your very own personal hard drive in the clouds that can be accessed anytime and anywhere.

Read on to learn more about why Cloud Drive makes the perfect storage space for you.

Cloud Drive – The Perfect Online Storage for You

With Cloud Drive services available to you, never worry about storing your important files and precious memories. Secure your 5 GB free storage on the cloud to store your photos, videos, files and all other documents in one place. The best part about storing your personal and precious belonging on cloud is accessibility. You can access all the things stored on the cloud on the go.

Amazon Cloud Drive is your solution if you want all your important data in one place where it can be accessed anytime and anywhere you are.

Your Storage Medium

Keeping your files protected in the cloud is as simple as moving your files to the Cloud Drive folder. Cloud Drive is your storage medium that has made storage simple. The Cloud Drive application can be downloaded and installed for both Mac and Windows.

Cloud Drive Photos for iPhone and Android is also available to download for simplifying the uploading procedure of photos from your tablet or phone so that you keep your precious memories with you without the fear of losing them. Even if your tablet or phone is damaged or lost, you can access all your important and precious data on the cloud.

If you are away from home or on the go and need to check out any file you stored in Cloud Drive earlier, you can use any of the above mentioned browsers to quickly access your file.

Accessibility at your Fingertips

Cloud Drive gives you the opportunity to access your files and photos wherever you are. Your important data and documents are always close at hand on your tablet, Android phone, iPhone or Kindle Fire.

The latest generation of Kindle Fire and Kindle Fire HD brings stored photos and documents on Cloud Drive within easy reach by providing you accessibility on the go. Use your tablet, Android phone or iPhone so you can check out your stored photos on the go by browsing Cloud Drive Photos

In addition to these advantages, the security of your photos, videos, files and other documents on Cloud Drive is an added benefit. Even when you lose or damage your tablet or phone, your data will be safe on the cloud, which you can access from your computer.

Your Computer and Cloud Drive

Exchanging Files Between Computer and Cloud

All important aspects of exchanging files between your computer and Cloud Drive will be covered in this section.

Uploading File to Cloud Drive Site

Upload files to Amazon Cloud Drive with your desktop application of Cloud Drive. You can also do so through a web browser on your personal computer.

The following steps will help you upload files to Cloud Drive from your computer:

Step 1 – Open Amazon Cloud Drive.

Step 2 – Click on the **Upload Files** option.

Step 3 – Click on **Your Cloud Drive** to choose a relevant destination folder to save your files. It is important to note here that if you forget to target a folder, the files uploaded will automatically go to Your Cloud Drive **root folder.** Once the files are successfully downloaded, they can be copied or moved into different folders respectively.

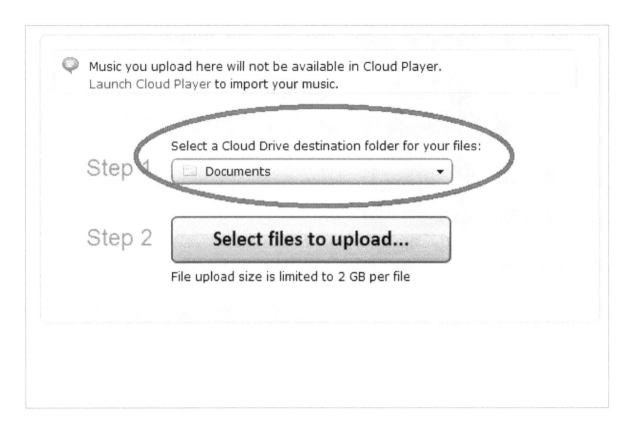

Step 4 – Click **Select Files to Upload** option.

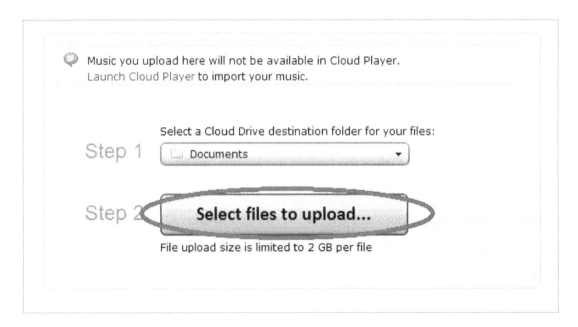

Step 5 – Select the specific file or the number of files you wish to upload to the Cloud Drive from your computer.

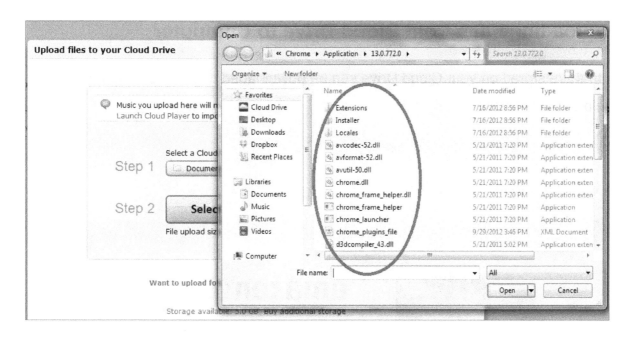

Step 6 – By confirming the selection you have made, the uploading will start instantly.

Downloading Files from Cloud Drive to Computer

Files that are stored on your Cloud Drive can be downloaded to your computer with the help of the following steps:

In order to download specific files directly from Cloud Drive:

Step 1 – Open Amazon Cloud Drive.

Step 2 – Check out the list of files on the Cloud Drive. Tick the check box right beside that option to download.

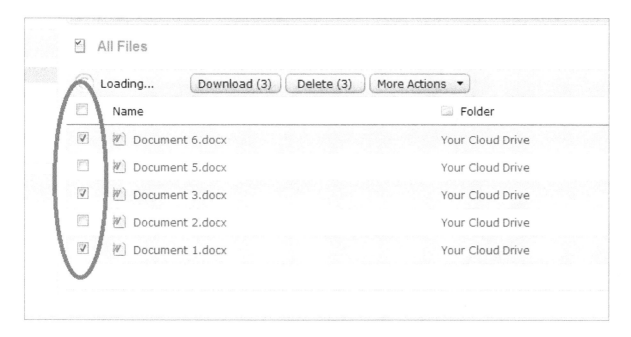

Step 3 – Click **Download** option to begin downloading.

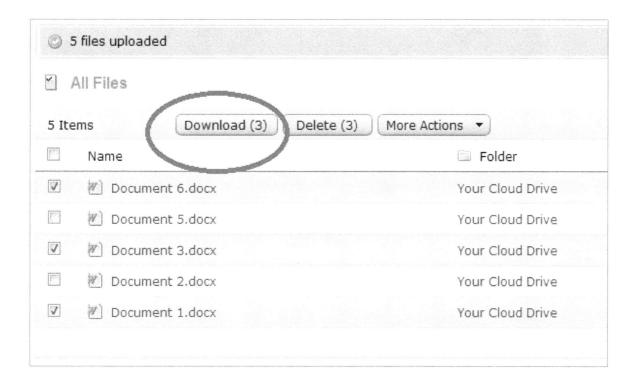

Step 4 – Check the on-screen instructions one by one and follow them thoroughly to download the file successfully.

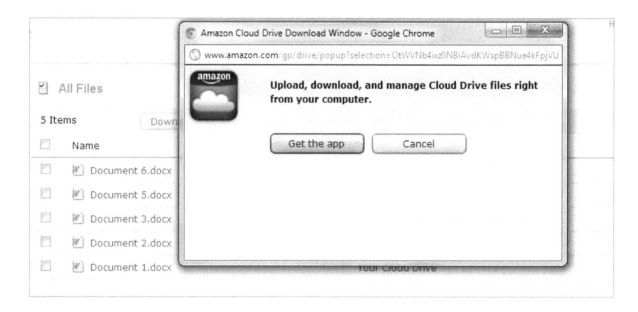

All Files

5 Items   Down...

Name

Document 6.docx

Document 5.docx

Document 3.docx

Document 2.docx

Document 1.docx

Cloud Drive File Management

You may wish to move, share or delete a file on Cloud Drive. Read on to find out how to do it.

Moving Your Files

You can move and reorganize your files and folders at Cloud Drive using your computer. To do so, follow the steps:

Step 1 – Open Amazon Cloud Drive.

Step 2 – Tick the check box in front of the files you wish to move.

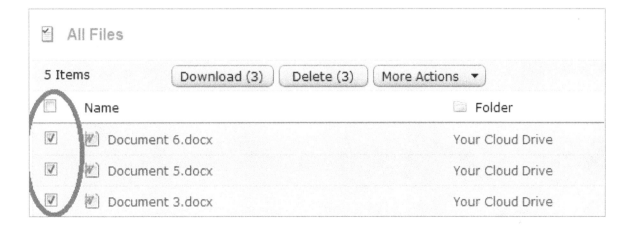

Step 3 – Select **More Actions** option.

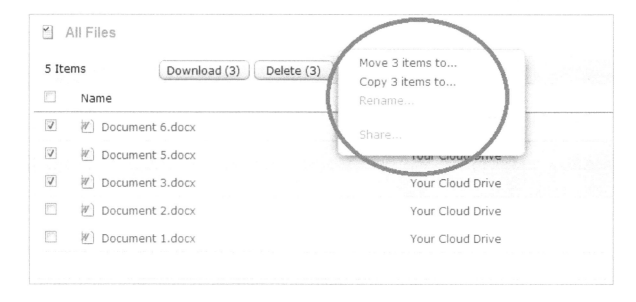

Step 4 – Click the 'move your file' option.

Step 5 – Chose the folder where you want to reorganize your files.

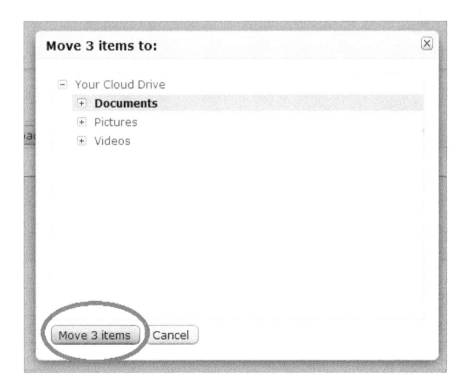

Step 6 – Finally, click **Move Items.**

Whatever changes you make in the Cloud Drive folder on your computer application will automatically be applied to the Cloud Drive website.

Sharing Your Files

It is possible to generate a URL or link for files stored in the Cloud Drive for the purpose of sharing it with anyone, anywhere.

Step 1 – Open Cloud Drive.

Step 2 – Tick the check boxes in front of the files you wish to share.

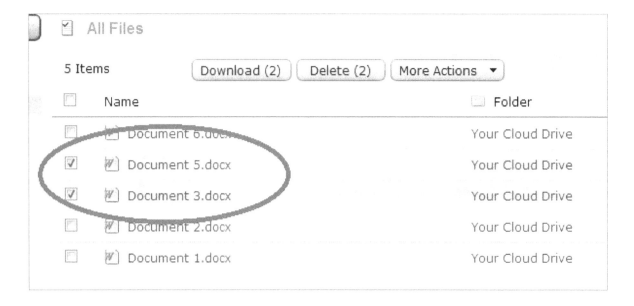

Step 3 – Check **More Actions** drop-down menu and click **Share.** A URL will be automatically generated. Copy the URL. Remember, all the files you are sharing can be seen in the **Shared Files** in your Cloud Drive.

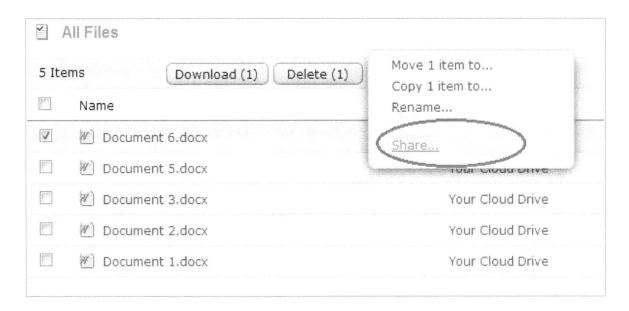

Step 4 – Share URL with anyone through email application or social media.

Note: Do not share private or sensitive information on Cloud Drive. The link you share can be further shared to other people.

Deleting a File

Files that are deleted from the Cloud Drive can be accessed in the **Deleted Items** folder. These files can also be restored, if required.

To delete a stored file in Cloud Drive, try one of the following methods:

- Open Amazon Cloud Drive in a web browser, tick mark the files you wish to delete and directly click the **Delete** button.

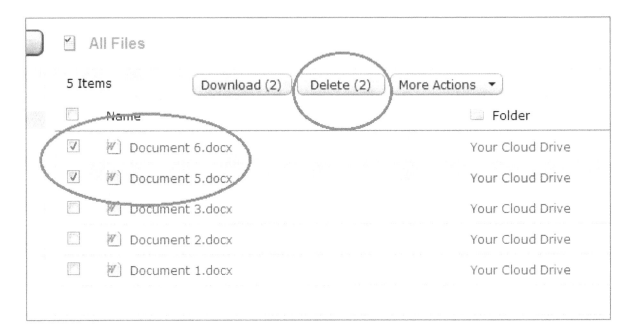

- Delete the file from the Cloud Drive window app installed in your computer.

Files are moved to **Deleted Items** before they can be permanently deleted.

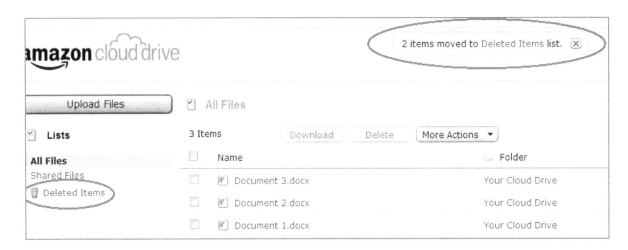

About Cloud Drive Desktop App

The desktop application available for Cloud Drive helps in files and folders management from your Mac computer or PC by simply downloading and installing Cloud Drive folder that automatically mirrors the website application.

The desktop application for Cloud Drive is compatible with Windows computers with Windows XP and above. Similarly, Mac Computers running Mac OS X 10.6 and above can run Cloud Drive desktop application successfully.

With the help of drag-and-drop technique, it is easy to upload and store files and folders to Cloud Drive without the need of opening the website.

Your Photos and Cloud Drive

For Android Application

Learn all that you want about Android Application for Cloud Drive Photos in this section.

About Cloud Drive Android App for Photos

Using an Android app for Cloud Drive Photos, you can access stored photos in Cloud Drive using your Android tablet or smartphone, or Kindle Fire first generation.

Downloading the App

Check out Google Play or Appstore from Amazon.com to download the Cloud Drive Photos for Android App.

Step 1 – Search Amazon Cloud Drive Photos from your device through Google Play or Amazon Appstore.

Step 2 – Tap to Download.

Step 3 – Follow instructions to use effectively.

Uploading Photos To Cloud Drive from Android

Use the app to upload photos to the Cloud Drive. You can also upload photos from the Android Gallery using your Android device.

From Android App:

Step 1 – Check out the list of photos in your android device.

Step 2 – Tap and hold the album or photo you wish to upload. If you are checking out photos individually, tap the menu option.

Step 3 – Tap **Upload to Cloud Drive.**

From Your Computer:

Step 1 – Go to Your Cloud Drive.

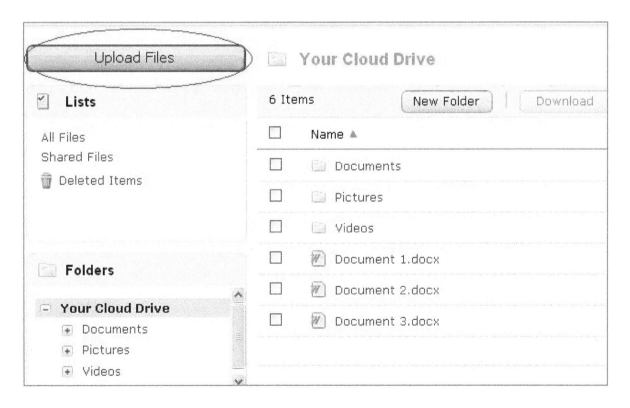

Step 2 – Click Upload.

Once uploaded successfully, your photos are securely stored on the Cloud Drive.

The photos can be easily accessed from the same platform.

For iPod Touch and iPhone Application

Store photos to Cloud Drive through iPhone and/or iPod Touch. Find out how!

About Cloud Drive iPod Touch and iPhone for Photos

With the Cloud Drive Photos for iPod touch and iPhone app, you can store and view photos on these devices, anywhere and at anytime.

Uploading photos to this app using the app itself or through your computer is easy. However, the benefits include accessing your photos anywhere you like as well as the security of your photos.

Downloading the App

Cloud Drive Photos is available at the Apple AppStore for iPod Touch and iPhone. This application supports iPhone 3GS and above.

To download the app:

Step 1 – Follow the link: https://itunes.apple.com/us/app/amazon-cloud-drive-photos/id621574163?ls=1&mt=8

Step 2 – Follow the instruction on screen to download.

Uploading Photos to Cloud Drive from iPod Touch and iPhone

Photos can be uploaded to your Cloud Drive Photos for iPod Touch and iPhone from the application itself as well as from your computer.

From the App:

Step 1 – Access photos stored in your device that you wish to store on Cloud Drive by tapping the device.

Step 2 – Open the photo you want to upload. **Actions** will appear by tapping the screen. Tap **Upload to Cloud Drive** from the options.

From Your Computer

Step 1 – Follow the link: http://www.amazon.com/clouddrive.

Step 2 – Click **Upload Files** to start uploading.

Remember: Your device's Camera Roll is automatically saved to your Cloud Drive through the Cloud Drive Photos for iPod Touch and iPhone app. To change the settings, go to **Settings** from the **Menu** and uncheck the box in front of **Automatically Save** option.

Cloud Drive Account

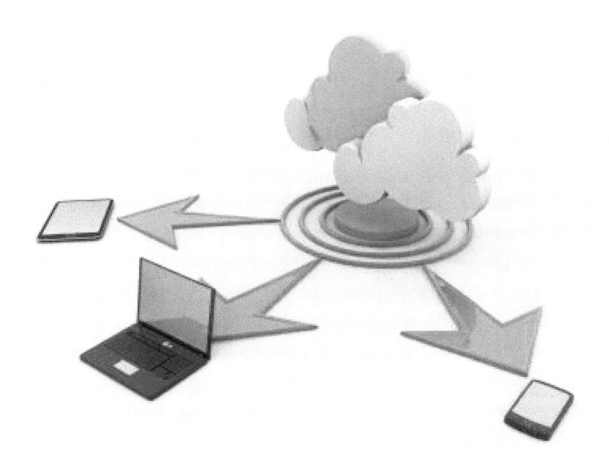

The Basics

Once you set up your account on Amazon Cloud Drive, you are eligible to use their free storage of up to 5 GB.

There are different data storage plans offered by Amazon to meet your personalized data storage requirements. You can check out the available options and choose to switch or upgrade your plan accordingly. Read on to learn more.

Remember: To begin your new experience at Cloud Drive, you must accept the **Terms of Use** of Cloud Drive.

Changing Storage Plan

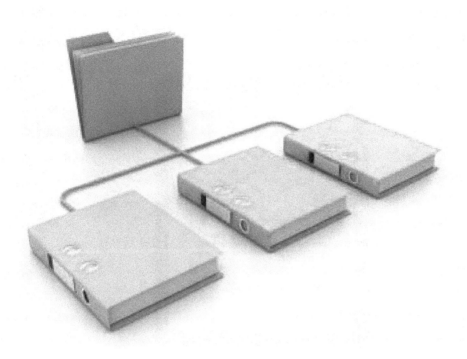

It is impossible to change your Cloud Drive storage plan according to your requirement. Choose a plan that meets your requirement more efficiently.

Important Information

A number of storage plan options are offered by Amazon to make your Cloud Drive experience more personalized and useful. When you upgrade or downgrade your existing plan, the new plan is instantly applicable.

If you are already operating on a paid storage plan, the upgraded charge will be adjusted with your last payment on a prorated basis. For instance, if there are 6 months still remaining on your current 20 GB package worth $10, at upgrading your subscription $5 will be instantly credited towards the upgrade.

On the other hand, by downgrading your current subscription, the remaining storage capacity is retained until the billing cycle ends. At the end of your billing cycle, your account will be downgraded to your new subscription plan.

If the uploaded data exceeds your current subscription plan limit, you are granted a limited amount of time to download the excess data and delete your files. However, you will not be allowed to upload any more files until the existing data is less than your current plan limit.

The Procedure

So how do you change your current subscription plan?

The capacity of storage is defined in kilobytes, megabytes and gigabytes. Follow the instructions to change your plan.

Step 1 – Follow the link: https://www.amazon.com/clouddrive/manage.

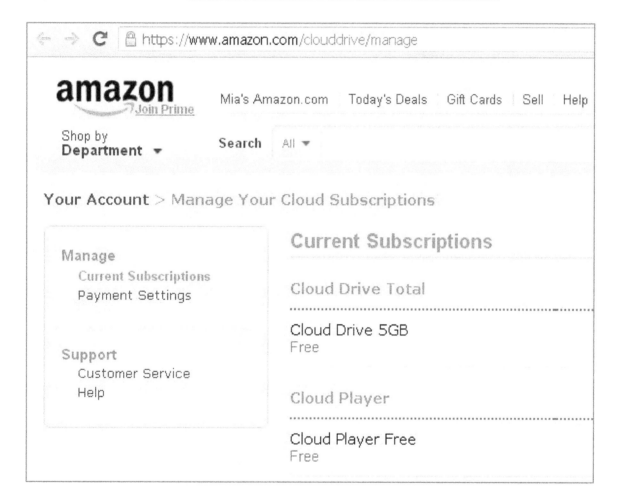

Step 2 – Check out the storage subscription options available and select the most suitable storage plan. You can **Upgrade** or **Downgrade** as per your own requirements.

Change Your Subscriptions
Select a different subscription and click Continue.
Cloud Player Premium provides storage for 250,000 imported songs. Cloud Player Free provides storage for 250 imported songs.
Your Amazon MP3 purchases do not count against these limits.

Files:

Your subscription
⊙ 5 GB
Free

○ 20 GB
$10.00 / year

○ 50 GB
$25.00 / year

○ 100 GB
$50.00 / year

○ 200 GB
$100.00 / year

○ 500 GB
$250.00 / year

○ 1000 GB
$500.00 / year

Step 3 – Choose a **payment method** to continue.

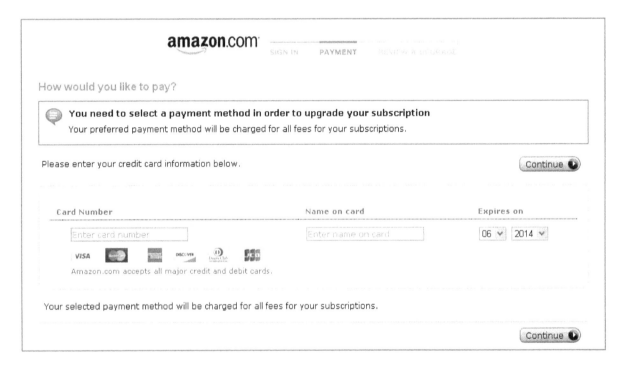

There is no limit as to how many times you can switch your subscription at Cloud Drive. In short, getting a bigger space in the 'cloud' is not difficult anymore.

Conclusion

Now that you have reached the last page of this book, you know the exact reason why getting your own space in the cloud is so important for the storage and security of your documents, files and photos.

With all the procedures mentioned step-by-step in detail, using Cloud Drive shouldn't be difficult anymore. Make the most out of your very own free 5 GB space available in the cloud and secure your important files and precious moments in photos on Cloud Drive secure storage.

www.ingramcontent.com/pod-product-compliance
Lightning Source LLC
Chambersburg PA
CBHW060511060326
40689CB00020B/4707